GEEZERBALL

GEEZERBALL

North Carolina Basketball at its Eldest

(Sort of a Memoir)

Richie Zweigenhaft

Half Court Press   Greensboro, NC

Copyright © 2020 by Richie Zweigenhaft
All rights reserved

First printing
ISBN 978-1-7329328-3-8

DESIGN. Text in Minion Pro. Titles in Fairfield LT. Cover and interior design by Andrew Saulters.

BACK COVER. The blurbs from Phil Jackson, David Stern, and Craig Chappelow are fake; the quote by Toni Kukoc is real.

This book is produced by Half Court Press, in cooperation with Scuppernong Books.

For Claire—
founding member of The Committee Meeting,
longtime participant in the Geezer Game,
valued colleague, and treasured friend

We do not quit playing because we grow old.
We grow old because we quit playing.

GEORGE BERNARD SHAW

GEEZERBALL

Chapters

1	Call Me Commish	3
2	Entering the Geezerhood	11
3	Participatory Autocracy	21
4	"Check Your Testosterone at the Door"	29
5	Off the Court	35
6	Some Reasons for the Game's Longevity	49

Appendices

1	My June 2003 Email to the Geezers	55
2A	"Guilford's Noontime Basketball" by Claire Morse	58
2B	"Order on the Court: A Lesson in Leadership" by Craig Chappelow	62
2C	"Men Score at Senior Games" by Rob Luisana	65
2D	"The Geezer Game and Dead Men Dribbling" by Richie Zweigenhaft	70
2E	"Geezer game: Playing together for 31 years" by Robert Bell	74

References	79
Acknowledgments	81
About the Author	85

GEEZERBALL

CALL ME COMMISH

CALL ME COMMISH. Some people do. I'm the organizer of a pickup basketball game that started in 1976, perhaps the longest running pickup game in North Carolina, or maybe even the nation. Who knows? A small group of us started playing, half-court, in 1976, in what is now called the old gym at Guilford College, the Quaker-affiliated school where I have been teaching since 1974. Just a few years before we started our game, future NBA players M. L. Carr and Lloyd Free (later known as World B. Free) had led the college's men's basketball team to the NAIA title, in that same gym, known as "The Crackerbox." It was the setting for many a basketball thrill.

My first year at Guilford was Lloyd Free's third and final year. He averaged 25.4 points per game, the team went 24-4, he was the NAIA player of the year, and he was drafted by Philadelphia in the second round of the NBA draft. Watching games that year in the Crackerbox (capacity: 933)[1], crammed in as we were like

---

1. The 933 figure is from Herb Appenzeller, *Pride in the Past*, published by Guilford College, 1987, p. 173. According to Appenzeller, the fire marshal set the capacity, and the basketball crowds in the Crackerbox were so large that a person was placed at the door with a clicker to count people off and to stop people from entering once capacity was reached.

the spectators at Indiana high school gyms portrayed in the movie *Hoosiers*, was the most exciting basketball I have ever seen.

I grew up in an era when those of us who were athletic played many sports. In the summer we played softball or baseball, we swam, we played golf and we played tennis. In the fall we played touch football (sometimes in the street). In the winter we played basketball. This was long before kids were encouraged or pressured to choose a particular sport. I was not a great athlete, but I played on my junior high school basketball and softball teams, and I played baseball and wrestled in high school. I liked basketball, but I was short (still am), and certainly had no sense that it would later become such a central part of my life.

From the time I was young, I liked racquet sports. My family had a much-used ping pong table in our house, and during the summers, especially at the overnight camp I attended from the time I was seven until I was 19, and then as a counselor for two years, I played a lot of tennis. In college, I learned to play squash. In California in the early 1970s, when one of my graduate school friends introduced me to racquetball, I fell in love with it. By the time I came to North Carolina in 1974 to teach at Guilford, I was playing racquetball four or five times a week. One of the first things I did after we moved to Greensboro was to scout out the local racquetball courts, and I soon found some guys to play with. For the first few years, I played about three times a week, and played in some local tournaments. I came in second in the city tournament in 1976, my racquetball peak.

When the small group of faculty and students began to play pick-up basketball in the Crackerbox we played just once a week. Soon we were playing twice a week, and, after a while, three times a week. Although I was a better racquetball player than basketball player, I enjoyed the basketball more—the game was more social, it called for more teamwork and strategy, and the interpersonal interactions were more complex. Eventually I was playing a lot of basketball and almost no racquetball.

More and more students and faculty joined the game. We had brief, sometimes very brief, appearances from other faculty, perhaps the original "one and done" players. A few administrators even showed up to play once or twice, but none lasted long. Bruce Stewart was one administrator who made a cameo appearance. Bruce left Guilford to become the Headmaster at Abington Friends and, from 1998 through 2009 he was the Headmaster at Sidwell Friends in Washington, D. C. He became a member of the Guilford College Board of Trustees in 1986, and the Chair of the Board from 1999 through 2003. He is the only member of the Board of Trustees ever to play in our game, though we extended an invitation to M. L. Carr, who was on campus periodically while he was on the Board from 1998 through 2009. At one point one of the guys in our game sent a letter inviting Barack Obama to play any time he came to North Carolina.

In the early days, we called our game "The Committee Meeting." This allowed us to avoid other mid-day commitments (for example, attempts by any of the committees I was on, such as the Curriculum Committee, to schedule a lunch meeting on a Monday, Wednesday or Friday). This ruse did not last for long, as everyone on campus soon knew of our dissembling—we even entered a team by that name in the college's intramural league. Decades later, I'm not sure when, I began jokingly to call it "The Geezer Game." Even though a few of the younger studs (relatively speaking of course) were offended by this term, it stuck.

This first era, from 1976 through 1981, for the most part a faculty-student half-court-game, ended when the college built the Ragan-Brown Field House in 1981. This kicked off a second era, during which the college began a twenty-year affiliation with the YMCA—the Y paid the college some amount of money, and Y members, including a coterie of basketball players, were allowed to use the facility. As the game moved from the Crackerbox to Ragan-Brown, gradually the number of those playing increased, and at some point we shifted from half-court to full-court. By the mid-1980s there were more non-Guilfordians playing noontime hoops than Guilford employees or students. By 2001 or so, there were enough players that we often had two, and sometimes three, full-court games running simultaneously. Over time, the games became more and more physical, not unlike the run-and-gun games you might find at any Y. To preserve the nature of our game—which historically had been competitive but less physical and less territorial than most pickup games—those of us from the college and those Y guys who preferred our "style" of basketball began to arrive early and we began to start our game on the most distant court from the entryway (court #3).

As a result, what had been a noon-time game gradually began at 11:45, and then, because more and more people came early, at 11:30. This meant that our game already had started when many of the bigger, faster, and mostly younger run-and-gun guys arrived. They would start a new game on court #1, and, as noted, some days there were enough players to start a third game on the middle court (court #2).

In November 2000, near the end of this second era, one of our regular players, Craig Chappelow, who works for the Center for Creative Leadership, wrote an article about our game in which he described the participants in the following way: "The group is a hodgepodge of former jocks and nonathletes from all professions. Last week my teammates consisted of an engineer, a podiatrist, an artist, and a guy who collects tractors."[2]

A key turning point took place in 2002 when a new branch of the YMCA, the Alex W. Spears III Family YMCA[3], was built just a few

---

2. Chappelow, Craig. 2000. "Order on the Court: A Lesson in Leadership." *Leadership in Action* 20(5):14.

3. Alexander W. Spears, III, was the CEO of Lorillard Tobacco Company from 1995 until 1999. He died of lung cancer in 2001. After Spears' death, the obituary in the local Greensboro paper was laudatory, even hagiographic, but the obituary in the *New York Times*, which emphasized his "unapologetic" claims that nicotine was not addictive and that "it has not been scientifically proven that smoking causes illness in humans," presented him in a far less favorable light. I recommend the 2016 documentary film, "Obit," about the obituary writers at the *New York Times*. The sometimes subtle but clearly political nature of obituaries is more widespread than many people realize, as I explored in an article in 2004 titled "Making Rags Out of Riches: Horatio Alger and the Tycoon's Obituary," in *Extra! The Magazine of FAIR—the Media Watch Group*, 17 (1):27-28.

miles away, and the college and the Y terminated their agreement. The Y members were told that they would no longer be able to use the college facilities, and they were encouraged to join the Spears YMCA. Some already had citywide Y memberships that allowed them to play at Spears, and others were willing to join Spears. However, many of the Y members who played regularly in our game (down on court #3) knew that we had something special, something that they were unlikely to find or recreate at the Y. They very much wanted to continue to play at Guilford, and those of us employed by Guilford who played in the game wanted them to be able to do so.

This, I now think, is when I began to take on the quasi-official role of Commissioner. I approached Brian Wenger, the guy who was then in charge of the facility, he directed me to the person he reported to in the administrative hierarchy, and he in turn sent the request further up the line. No one was sure whether the non-Guilford employees should be allowed to continue to play at Guilford, or under what conditions. One main concern was liability, but another was whether they should pay, and, how much. Finally, I was told, it got to the college's then relatively new President, Kent Chabotar, and, in a very wise move on his part, he allegedly (I was not there) said, "Sure, let them keep playing."[4] The

---

4. I have no doubt that by the time Kent Chabotar stepped down from the presidency in 2014, I was perceived by some as one of his more outspoken critics. Although I thought he was quite capable when it came to some aspects of his job, I did at times publically criticize certain actions that he and his administration took. For example, when the college, with minimal faculty input, and certainly without faculty approval, accepted a ten-year grant from the BB&T Foundation that stipulated that some students would be required to read Ayn Rand's *Atlas Shrugged*, the lengthy polemical novel that has taken on biblical dimensions for some right-wing thinkers, a book that endorses individualism, justifies selfishness, and idealizes capitalism, I wrote an article in 2010 that was published in *Academe* titled "Is This Curriculum for Sale?" Despite such public criticisms, I believe that Kent had clear strengths, and some very good moments—his decision to allow the off-campus geezers the ability to continue playing in the midday game was one of his best (though he might not place it near the top of his list).

deal that ultimately was reached was that I, like one of the coaches, could "rent" the court for three hours a week, at the discount rate of $27 per hour that the coaches paid for the various camps that they ran, especially during the summer. Thus, for $81 a week, or, about $4,000 a year, we could rent the court.

Although some players arrived by 11:30, the game usually began by 11:45, and we typically played until about 1, it was agreed that we could pay for only one hour per day, three times a week. No one has questioned this. In fact, during some periods in the 17 years since this system went into effect (especially periods of extensive administrative turn-over), I'm not sure if anyone would have noticed if I stopped paying completely.

Therefore, in an email to the non-Guilfordians I explained that if they paid me what was likely to be about $300 per year (much less than the cost of joining Spears) that we should have enough money to cover the rental of the court; I did not ask those employed by the college to pay anything on the grounds that access to the field house was a perquisite that came with their employment (see Appendix 1 for that email explaining our options; it also includes a list of those who received the email, the "charter members" of the post-2003 game).

This was the start of the third era (what might be considered our "modern era"). Now, 16 years later, we are still renting the court (same cost—no inflation yet), and so this now 27-year-old game got past this institutional hurdle in 2003. We pay $810 every ten weeks. The college provides a court, shower facilities, and most years, towels (some years we have had to bring our own). It has from my point of view definitely been a win-win.

There have been ups and downs, smooth and not so smooth periods, some new players who fit in nicely to the game, and some who have not fit in so well. There have been many rule changes proposed, and some adopted; there have been arguments, with players walking off the court in anger; and there even have been fights. For the most part, the game has endured with relatively few major problems. We are definitely older, and maybe wiser.

How is it that this pickup game has lasted more than 40 years? What have we done that has allowed for such longevity? There are I am sure many factors at play, but I think that three guiding principles have been especially important. The first is that everyone gets to play an equal amount. The second is that we try our best to keep injuries and arguments to a minimum. And the third is based on the slogan that the Chinese used during the Cold War: "Friendship First, Competition Second." This slogan became known to Americans when, after more than twenty years during which the two countries had neither diplomatic nor economic relations, an American table tennis team was invited to visit Communist China in 1971. My wife, Lisa, still says "friendship first" to me when I leave the house to play ball.

ENTERING THE GEEZERHOOD

MUCH AS I RESPECT democratic voting procedures, and the value of consensus (especially here in Quakerland), in the geezer game we rarely take votes and we typically don't achieve consensus in the traditional Quaker way. (I'll note, parenthetically, that having worked at a Quaker-affiliated college for more than four decades, "achieving consensus in the traditional Quaker way" is not as clear-cut a concept as it might sound).

In that initial email that I sent to 30 players, back in June 2003 (see Appendix 1),[1] I laid out my willingness to oversee the game but my unwillingness to try to run a parliamentary or traditional Quaker meeting. I wrote the following:

---

1. Nine of the 30 recipients of that email are still playing: Craig Chappelow, Thom Espinola, Rusty Hoffman, Ron Irons, Charlie Johnson, Dan Lenze, Danny McCoy, Steve Schlehuser, Bob Williams, and me. Two are on the extended disabled list but allege that they are coming back (Rob Luisana and Bob Wineburg). One has a new job and has been unable to play for most of the last six months, but shows up periodically, and is still therefore part of the geezerhood (Greg Mayer). At least three have died (thankfully, not on the court): George Cox, Robert Pearse, and Darryl Rolandelli.

I'm sure that there will be decisions to make along the way about membership and other matters. My plan is to make these decisions myself, unless I want or need help. If I do, then I will draw on a Guilford College Interdisciplinary Basketball-Playing Faculty Kitchen Cabinet consisting of Thom Espinola (physics), Claire Morse (psychology) and Bob Williams (economics). In addition, I'm assuming that at times, I'll poll all paying members (to decide, for example, whether to include a new person in the game, or, just to come up with a wild example, whether to ban someone who makes the mistake of starting a fight or throwing the ball in someone's face).

Over the many years of the game, we have, of course, lost players. Some have moved away, some have changed jobs and no longer can play midday, some have what we think of as "career-ending injuries," and, as I have noted (well, footnoted), a few have died.

So, too, have we added players. Typically, someone has heard about the game, one of our current players has a friend or a colleague who is interested in playing, or the college has hired a new employee who wants to play. When this happens, I ask the potential new player to call or email me, I arrange to meet with them (often over coffee or beer), I explain the game to them, including the rules we use, the culture of the game, and the costs for those not employed by Guilford. For many years we had a Sunday game at a local high school, and we had the option of trying people out in that game before making a commitment to allow them in our game, but the Sunday game has faded (long story).

For the most part we have operated on the assumption that the game is for older, not younger, players, though over the years we have moved the cut-off point upwards. Mostly I recall saying that we should not allow anyone to join the game who is under 40 and, if we make exceptions, they have to promise to pass the ball and play defense. Right now, among the active players, the oldest is 78, and the youngest is 39. The average age is 61.7: in addition to the one guy still in his late thirties, three are in their 40s, six in their 50s, seven in their 60s, and four in their 70s. (The Commissioner is 74). Of course, by the time you read this, if all goes well, we all will be older.

Currently all of the geezers are male. Claire Morse, my wonderful colleague in the psychology department for many years, played in the game from its inception in 1976 until she retired from teaching, and from the geezer game, in 2011. Other women periodically have played in the game, including, at times, members of Guilford's women's basketball team during their off-season. In an article that she wrote in 1985 about "The Committee Meeting," Claire concluded: "These men are comrades of a special sort, and our shared play can certainly lead me to respect and enjoy them from the perspective of a woman who has been allowed to participate simply as another player in a game we all enjoy."[2]

Here is what might be a typical example of how we decided to let a guy in the game. It took place back in 2006, when we were still trying to figure out what procedure to follow. Rob Luisana, the owner of an insurance agency who began to play in our game in the late 1980s, wrote an article for the local paper about a group of our geezers who had participated in a three-on-three tournament at East Carolina University, part of the North Carolina Senior Games. Not long after that, Mike R., a guy who read the article, showed up at the Guilford gym to watch us play. He talked with one of our players, Bob Wineburg, who wrote me about him ("He is 6' 5" and seems nice. He hasn't played in a year and would like to know what the procedure is to get in the game."). Bob gave me the guy's email, I wrote him, and we arranged to meet for coffee. I liked him, and thought he'd be a nice addition to the game, so I sent an email to the geezers, asking their approval. After numerous humorous emails (one wrote, "Don't forget the criminal background check," another

2. Morse, Claire. 1985. "The Committee Meeting: Guilford's Noontime Basketball." *Guilford Review* 22(Fall):19.; see Appendix 2A.

wrote, "I vote yes... but prefer to run his credit and get a financial statement!!!," and a third wrote, "Since I'd love for someone else to cover Ron, I vote 'yea'"), Craig Chappelow wrote a longer, (mostly) more serious, reply. It included the following:

> OK, you guys have had your fun. The commissioner has asked for your serious input, which he didn't have to do, and he gets some kind of comedy routine back in return. I think the only way to do this is to let the new guy "naked walk" down the hall to the shower. If Guilford receives any student complaints about lumps, scars, or body hair—he's in!
>
> OK, serious answer. I think the question is as much about a process for considering new folks as it is about this Mike guy. Some alternatives below. I could live with any of them, but my preference would be the first.
>
> 1. Let the numbers drive openings for new people. Right now the numbers are great—always enough, seldom too many. If adding new people means I would end up on half court more, I'd vote no. But if a regular were to leave, then we would add to balance the numbers.
>
> 2. Let Richie decide. He knows what we're looking for and could probably get a sense quick enough. Downside is if the guy turns out to be a Biff [a former player from the pre-Spears days, big trouble], I would also be looking to Richie to deal with the problem.
>
> 3. Let the guy play free for a few days and then have some quick discussion and decision among the regulars.
>
> Open to any other suggestions. No more engineers please.

We let him play. He was a nice addition. Unfortunately, after playing only four times, he wrote to tell me that his back was giving him too much trouble, and he could no longer play ("I am going to have stop with the basketball. The back can't just handle it—the problems are different but in the same area.").

This pretty much set the pattern as various people have asked to join the game over the years. Some, like Mike R., only played a few times before disappearing for one reason or another. Others we let in the game and they have become regular participants. Some we decided against.

A trickier or at least different issue has emerged as people who work at the college have asked about joining us. I have argued that we should include them, in part because I believe that for the game to endure we need the support of administration and staff. This has meant that even though some of those who have asked to play have been younger than 40, or didn't exactly play the game we like (that is, they played a more physical game or a more run-and-gun game, they were less likely to pass the ball, and less likely to play defense), we have in every case said yes. For example, at one point, a staff member who had been playing in the game for a while (Rex), asked if his boss (Jon) could join the game.

Here is what I wrote to the geezers about this request:

Geezers,

Rex mentioned to me last Wednesday that his boss...whose official title is something like Associate Vice President of Operations and Facilities, has expressed interest in playing with us in the noontime game. I told Rex that I was going out of town, and that I would contact Jon when I got back. I want to touch base with you first.

I'm ambivalent, but lean toward letting him in. He was supportive when I first approached the administration about us renting the gym (though, ultimately, it was the support of Kent Chabotar, the President, that settled the matter). In no small part because he is in charge of all facilities on campus, I think the long-term health of the game might be enhanced by allowing him to play (and it might not be enhanced if we don't let him to play, though that may not be the case).

[Jon] looks to be about 40 or so, maybe a bit older, and I have not seen him play...I think it is the right thing to do to allow not just full-time faculty but also full-time staff to play in the game—we faculty already have many privileges compared to many others who work at the college, and I am uncomfortable saying that faculty can play but staff cannot.

Let me know what you think. I plan to contact Jon within a day or two.

RICHIE

We let Jon in, and he played for a number of years until his sudden departure from the college (about which the rumors are still flying). Although some of the big guys who had to cover him might not agree with me, I think he was a net plus, in no small part because he let us into the gym on days when the college was officially closed, and apparently he was instrumental in arranging to have a court named after me when I turned 70 (more on that to come).

So, too, did I approach the geezerhood about another staff member, Mark, who at the time he asked to join the game was only 35 years old. Here is the email I wrote to them before we let him in the game:

Geezers,

We have a request to join the game from Mark..., who has been a full-time employee at Guilford College for the past two months (he is the Interim Director of ITS). He heard about the game (Rex), emailed me about playing, and I met with him today. I explained to him the history of the Geezer Game (the short version—10 minutes or so), and some of the rules that have evolved over the years (e.g., Half Court Monday—I didn't include the history of whether to call backcourt or not, or how we deal with balls that hit the wire above the backboard). I emphasized that we try to avoid conflicts, both physical and verbal, and that we have various strategies to do so (e.g., not having to win to stay on the court, calling jump balls instead of trying to resolve disagreements). He seemed to understand.

One possible glitch is that he is younger than 40—he is only 36. He assures me that he is out of shape and feels older. He was sitting down, so I am not sure how tall he is, but I could see that he is not a point guard and that he has a pretty good size spare tire on him. He did not play high school or college ball, but has played pickup, industrial league, and he has coached both children and teenagers. Just from looking at him, I'd say that if I had to assign him someone to cover, I'd have him cover Steve the Really Elder or Danny (not Andy, Chris, Bob Williams, Tim, or Thom). He has not played in the last six months. I suggested to him that if we let him play, he begin with Half Court Monday, though I informed him that we had not played full court in a while.

I explained to him that permission would be needed from the geezerhood, and that I would get back to him after I had emailed you. I recommend that we let him in, despite his youth. Among other things, my department and I depend greatly on computers, and I need to maintain good relations with those who work in ITS.

Please let me know if you have objections. If I don't hear any within a few days, I'll invite him to join us one of these Mondays...

RICHIE

So, that is our system, such as it is. I consult with the geezerhood, but ultimately I decide (participatory autocracy?). For the most part this has worked.

How Much Do They Pay To Play?

AS I HAVE INDICATED, since 2003 we have been renting the court, and the fee from the college has not changed, nor has the fee for the geezers increased until recently. The payment system I have put in place is that the geezers pay me, either the full fee for the entire year, with a discount (the optimists) or two payments due in January and July, for the first and second six months of the year (the pessimists). Until recently, the optimists were given a slight discount (and paid $275) and the pessimists made two payments of $150. Because we recently had a drop in our numbers (due to injuries and a few people changing to new jobs that interfered with their basketball schedule), I increased the annual fee from $300 to $350—the optimists who paid for the entire year still received a discount, and paid only $300, and the pessimists paid two installments of $175.

Inevitably, adjustments needed to be made when guys got hurt and were out for long periods of time or had new jobs that allowed them only to play once in a while, or, in a few cases, only played in the summer. I have allowed part-time participants to play for $5 per day, using an honor system—they keep track, and at the end of the year they pay me whatever the total comes to. For example, the college houses the Eastern Music Festival every summer. For a few years, Calvin J., one of the administrators in that program, who came to Greensboro from his home in Florida for six weeks or so, saw us playing and asked if he could join us. We let him play, and I arranged for him to pay $5 for each day that he played (as a result, we pulled in $30 in 2006, and $25 in 2007). So, too, with Steve H., an alum who played regularly in our game when he was a student and continued to play for a number of years after he graduated while he still lived in Greensboro. He now lives in Maryland, but he shows up every few summers, and plays for a week or two. Another guy, Cliff M., accumulates so much leave time where he works that late in the calendar year he has to take some days off or lose them; for the last few years, he has been able to play 10-12 times, almost always on Fridays in November and December, and sometimes during the year on holidays when the company he works for is closed but the college is open. Tim M. played for about a year, and then moved to Hawaii, but during the summer when he visits family in Greensboro he plays in the game. The fact that these players return when they are in town or come back to play when their work schedules allow, speaks to the long-term appeal of the game—people hate to give it up, just as the regulars hate to miss playing on the days that they can't. Though at the time of the 2019 increase from $300 to $350 one geezer raised questions about whether Guilford employees should have to pay to play, and about whether the $5 system for those who could not play often was fair to those who paid full freight, this system has mostly gone without challenge or problems.

I have an excel file which shows who paid, how much they paid, and the date on which they paid. It allows me to keep track of "delinquents," those who are more than a few weeks late in their payments—I send them reminder emails when necessary. I keep the money in an account at my bank, and I write checks to Guilford College every ten weeks for $810. Each year, we have had a little left over, and some years we have given Christmas gifts to the administrator in charge of the facility. One year we bought a fancy digital clock for the college and, under it, on the wall next to the court that we usually play on, we arranged for a plaque that says it was given to the college by the geezers. The plaque includes the following quote by George Bernard Shaw: "We do not quit playing because we grow old. We grow old because we quit playing."

PARTICIPATORY AUTOCRACY

WHEN IT COMES to figuring out the rules we play by, I have used this same somewhat autocratic approach that draws on consultation and sometimes even achieves consensus. When I told one of the geezers that I was writing about how the game had lasted so long, and I mentioned the phrase, "participatory autocracy," he reminded me that Bruce Springsteen made a similar decision early in the life of the E Street Band—Bruce told the others in the band that he wanted input from them, but ultimately he was going to make the key decisions about the music, about the performances, and about the marketing. Bruce's power over the lives of those in the E Street Band was much greater than whatever influence I have had over the geezers, and, accordingly, whereas I use the phrase "participatory autocracy" he uses the phrase "benevolent dictatorship." Here is part of how he explained his role with the band: "I didn't want to get into any more decision making squabbles or have any confusion about who set the creative direction of my music....I look back on this as being one of the smartest decisions of my young life....I crafted a benevolent dictatorship: creative input was welcome within the structure I prepared..."[1] I am not sure that this is the best way to go about keeping a pickup basketball game going, or that all groups would accept participatory autocracy, but this has worked pretty well for us (and the benevolent dictatorship has worked for Bruce and the E Street Band).

Winners Up?

ONE OF OUR guiding principles has been that everyone should get to play, and another has been that we should strive to reduce the deleterious effects of territoriality. On many courts the prevailing system is "winners up." That is, when there are extra players, the first one to arrive who is not in the game calls next game ("I got next"), and that person forms a team (sometimes simply by choosing teammates from the players on the team that lost and any others waiting to play, sometimes based simply on who is waiting and the order in which they arrived, sometimes based on shooting foul shots). The team that won the previous game stays on the court. This, of course, puts an even greater premium on winning. I have no doubt that arguments are more likely to occur and fights are more likely to break out when people are playing to keep the court. Moreover, no one wants to have to sit and watch others play (especially in a noon-time game when many have to get back to work). Though newcomers sometimes suggest it, we never have played winners up.

Therefore, the system we use is that with an even number of players (6, 8, or 10), we simply make teams and play, trying, as best we can, to make even teams so the games will be close. Typically, I make the teams. If I am late, or if I am not there, someone else does. In his November 2000 article about the game, Craig Chappelow wrote the following: "Everyone looks to Richie to divide the players into teams to get the games started—not because the rest of us can't

1. Springsteen, Bruce. 2016. *Born to Run*. New York, NY: Simon and Schuster.

but because Richie has an uncanny knack for setting up balanced teams. Dan McCoy, a mortgage banker and lunch league regular, points out that 'Richie would enjoy nothing more than a three-game split with the scores 15 to 13." [2] Danny McCoy was right: I do want close games. My ideal day has the two teams splitting the first two games (both of which are close), with the third game decided when I hit the game-winning shot, preferably a three.

If we have an odd number, say 7, 9 or 11, one team gets an extra player, and that team rotates that player in and another player out every 10 points. If we have 12 players, each team has six, and the two teams each rotate a player out every 10 points (usually two people who are guarding each other go out together, though this does not always work based on when people have arrived); if we have 13 players, then one team has 7, the other 6, and every 10 points the seven-person team rotates two people out, while the six-person team rotates one person out. This is one of the cases when we have had on-court votes. With 13, there is the question of whether to play one five-on-five game (rotating three people in and out) or two three-on-three games (with a sub in one of the games). Some of us (this includes me), following the principle that no one wants to sit, have argued for two games; others, who hate to play three-on-three, prefer the five-on-five game with a three-person rotation. For a while we voted, but after three votes in a row in which the group chose to play one game, not two, we stopped taking votes at 13 (though there are still, periodically, calls for a vote, and some geezers might be shifting in their view on this).

With the arrival of a 14th person, we used to just split into two games, sometimes asking the latest arrivals to play in the three-on-three game, not the four-on-four game. Again, some people balked, and in fact, one guy left the gym in anger one day rather

---

2. Chappelow, Craig. 2000. "Order on the Court: A Lesson in Leadership." *Leadership in Action* 20(5):15.

than be demoted to the three-on-three game (the three-on-three game has at times been referred to as the "J. V. game"). For a period, we voted whether to play one or two games when we had 14, but the voting process was surprisingly laborious (some people abstained, some half raised their hands), and resistance remained. The policy that has evolved for the time being at least is that I ask if six people are willing to play three-on-three (me and five others). If so, those volunteers head to the other end of the court and play three-on-three, leaving the remaining eight to play four-on-four (if another person arrives, #15, that person rotates into the larger game; if #16 arrives, we have two four-on-four games). This is as good an example as any of the realization that my above-mentioned "somewhat autocratic approach" is only "somewhat"— one can only ignore the wishes of the people to a certain extent or rebellion takes place.

One more thing to negotiate is when to add players into an ongoing game. Many of those in our game come to play during their lunch hours, and their work responsibilities mean that some people drift in shortly or well after we have started the first (or even the second) game. Some always arrive early. Some are chronically late. One player, let's call him John Smith, always comes late so he is generally referred to as "the late John Smith." If we have just started, or if we are midway through the game, no problem, we add late arrivals. If, however, we are close to the end of the game, especially if it is a close game, we sometimes make the latecomer wait until the game ends. It is yet another subjective decision, one that sometimes I make, and sometimes is made by a quick effort at on-court consensus.

Make it Take it?

SIMILARLY, MANY, MAYBE most, pickup games go by what is called "make it, take it," which means that (unlike real games, with officials and clocks) after a basket is made the team that just scored gets the ball again. This allows the stronger team to win the game quickly, conceivably without the losing team ever getting the ball. In an attempt to avoid lopsided games, we have never played "make it, take it."

How Many Points Per Game?

FOR MANY YEARS, we played games to 15, each basket counting as one point, but you had to win by two (which led to some memorable overtime games that went well into the high 20s, maybe even the low 30s). In 2006, a subgroup began to play in The Senior Games, an annual three-on-three tournament held at East Carolina University, and in that tournament they used the three-point line. The first year we played, we realized that they scored the way most high schools, colleges, and the pros did: regular baskets counted as two points, shots from behind the three-point line as three points, and foul shots as one point. In 2007, for a month or so prior to going back to ECU for a second year, we began to use the three-point line at Guilford to practice our outside shots and to prepare for the tournament's scoring system. We changed the scoring system from games to 15, with each basket counting one point, to games to 30, with threes counting three and other baskets counting two (we don't shoot foul shots). People seemed to like this, maybe in part because it mirrored "real" basketball, so we have stuck with it. We did not keep the win-by-two rule, so we no longer have the possibility of overtime games.

Full Court or Half Court?

FOR MORE THAN 30 years, if we had only six or seven players, we played half court, but if we had eight or more, we played full. In December 2012, Danny McCoy, who started playing in the game in 1986, concluded that playing full-court was becoming too hard on his body. He proposed that we designate one day a week to play half court, thinking that he would play on that day but not on the other two days. He submitted a written proposal to the Commissioner, and the Commissioner flew it by the geezerhood. In my email to them, I wrote that "Given the number of knee braces worn on any given day, not to mention the number of geezers who are battling one aging or injury related issue or another, I think this proposal has merit." The geezers either agreed, or, at least, they did not disagree vehemently. The two physicians in the game, both high energy, and both a good bit younger than the average geezer, were resistant; one of them wrote, "I am officially not for it but understand why there would be interest in it." We did not have unanimous support. If we had really been running a Quaker meeting, and I was the Clerk, I would have asked these two if they were willing to "stand aside," which means that they would be willing to allow the decision to go forth but that they wished for their disagreement to be recorded. It was not a Quaker meeting, it was participatory autocracy, so I simply made the decision. Thus began a period known as "Half Court Mondays." For the next year or two, we always played half court on Monday, no matter how many players showed up, but on Wednesdays and Fridays, if we had eight or more players, we played full-court. One of the geezers even arranged for t-shirts that said "Half Court Monday: Half a Workout Since 2012."

One day while I had rotated out of a full-court game, I observed a few of the younger players racing up and down the court while the others watched, and I also observed lots of wild passes thrown out of bounds on aborted fast breaks. I could see that the full-court game had become ragged, and based on these observations, and comments from some geezers, I concluded that for most of us the full-court game was less fun than the half-court game. Either I suggested, or others did, that we just play half court all the time. Except for a few of the younger guys, there was general agreement. We have not played full-court in six or seven years.

A Foul or a Charge? Out on Me or Out on You?
Did that Ball Hit the Line? Walking?
The Strategic Use of Jump Balls.

KEEPING ARGUMENTS TO a minimum is one of our guiding principles. As anyone who has played pickup basketball, or anyone who has watched high school, college or pro basketball, knows, when an offensive player and a defensive player collide, they, their teammates, and the fans are not likely to agree on whether it was a foul or a charge. In pickup games, although there sometimes are long and heated discussions about this, rarely if ever is either player persuaded that the other is right. In college and the NBA these days, there are long stretches while the referees review tapes to try to determine just what happened. To avoid such discussions, and the ill-will they inevitably cause, and to keep the game moving, we have put a simple procedure in place: if there is a disagreement (about a charge, or about whether a ball hit the out of bounds line, or anything else) we try to keep the discussion to a minimum—we simply call it a jump ball, we rotate possession, and we keep playing.

Similarly, to keep arguments to a minimum, we encourage everyone to "respect the call" (at one point we also had a set of geezer t-shirts with "Respect the call" on the back). In some pickup games, only the person on offense can make a call. We encourage either player to make a call. That is, if you foul me, I can call it, but so, too, can I call it if I foul you (not only "can I," I should). There is no penalty for fouls (we don't take the time to shoot foul shots, as they apparently do, or once did, in a pickup game at the Winston-Salem YMCA), so there is no real deterrent to fouling someone, and some take advantage of this. I have at times sent emails to certain players encouraging them to foul people less frequently (and in some cases, less aggressively). These have been received with differing responses. One guy who received such an email (what the Quakers would call an "eldering" email) wanted to argue that we should then be more open to offensive fouls, because, he claimed, on some of the fouls that had been called against him he actually had been fouled. Another recipient of one of my eldering emails was offended enough that he disappeared for two years. Mostly, however, people try not to foul too much, or, if they do, they are given sufficient grief by those on the court to deter them from continuing to do so.

"CHECK YOUR TESTOSTERONE AT THE DOOR"

WE DO HAVE arguments now and then. People yell at each other, and, in some cases, walk off the court—sometimes to avoid saying something they regret or to prevent their anger from escalating to a physical confrontation.

In two incidents that took place a few years apart, when they reached a certain level of anger, two different geezers yelled "Suck my dick" at the person who angered them (it was the same person—no surprise there, as he has angered many people). I find it interesting that when they got this angry these ostensibly macho guys chose such a homoerotic phrase. Such outbursts, however, are rare.

We have had only three physical confrontations in our 44 years. The first happened long ago, either in 1981 or 1982. My memory of it is hazy, though I know it took place upstairs in the Crackerbox, and the perpetrator was a visiting professor in Economics on a two-year appointment whose game was more aggressive than we were used to. Something set him off, or, as is often the case, an accumulation of things set him off, and he went after the guy who was covering him. It didn't last long, we admonished him, and soon he was no longer at Guilford, so we did not have to deal with him, nor did we have to deal with actual fighting for about thirty years.

Then, in May 2011, we had another incident. It took place on a day when we had enough players for two games, and I was in the game on the other court. Suddenly I heard commotion from the other game, and I saw a bunch of guys gathered around two of our younger, more athletic players, who were tangled up on the floor, clearly in the midst of a fight. People pulled them apart, and I told them both to leave. One in particular wanted to explain to me what had happened, for he was quite sure that he was not at fault (as Bruce Springsteen says to a judge in the long introduction to one of his songs, "Guilty with an explanation"), but I was not interested in holding a trial at that time on the court. I told him I'd do some thinking and be in touch.

They left. We finished the games. I got a lot of advice in the locker room, some serious, some not, and in fact did spend a few hours thinking about what the most appropriate response might be. I then sent the following email to all the geezers:

Geezers,

I sent the tapes to David Stern, and he got back to me immediately.

No suspensions, but a warning to everyone. We not only need to respect the call, but in general we need to have less needling, less yapping, less trash talking, and less arguing. I know that all of these things are part of the give and take of pickup basketball, but they also can contribute to the accumulation of antagonism. I have no doubt that the altercation that took place today had its origins in games that have been played over the last few weeks or months, and was not caused simply by whatever took place on court #1.

Those of you who still are young enough to have a lot of testosterone need to check some of it at the door.

If you find yourself getting especially frustrated or angry, just call it a day and leave the game rather than letting your frustration or anger escalate. Over the years we have had very very few conflicts that have led to actual physical confrontations... but periodically various players have been frustrated or angry enough to leave early (including your commish, once—yes, it was Wineburg). In other basketball settings it might make sense to stand your ground (for example, if your coach is named Krzyzewski), but given the spirit of the geezer game it is better for you and for the long-term health of the game to call it a day.

So, no suspensions, but everyone is on probation.

RICHIE

*****A commissioner's work is never done*****

This email seemed to stem the tide.[1] But then, just about two years later, in April 2013, we had another confrontation, two different guys, not really a fight—one took a swing at another, and connected.

The two involved in this altercation had both played football in high school. The aggressor, who was about 5'11" and 200 pounds, was covering a bigger man, about 6'2" and 240. Apparently things were getting increasingly heated between them, which I had not noticed. If I had, I might have made a defensive shift so they wouldn't have continued to cover each other. I am not sure how long it took for things to escalate to the point of no return, but we were all stunned when a fist was thrown and contact was made, though I think the fist made contact with the recipient's shoulder, not his face. If, as I believe, Bruce Hornsby is correct when he sings in his classic song about pickup basketball, "Take Me to the old Playground," that "how you play is who you are," then it can be said with confidence that the guy who took the swing, now a former geezer, is prone to impulsivity, and is likely to act without a great deal of premeditation.

---

1. Both are still in the game.

I told the guy who threw the punch to leave, and that I'd be in touch. He did, though after we finished playing, he came into the locker room to apologize. I said that we couldn't have fights in the geezer game, and that I'd let him know what the penalty would be. That afternoon, I wrote him an email telling him that he was suspended for a week. Here is the email I sent to him:

XXXXX,

We've been playing midday basketball here at Guilford for 37 years now, and we've had our share of conflict, arguments, hurt feelings, and people walking off the court angry. Including the confrontation that took place earlier today, we have had very few actual physical confrontations. The previous confrontation took place in May 2011. I am concerned about the quality of the game, and I am concerned about the safety of the (old and getting older) geezers who play, and therefore I don't think we can take today's event lightly. My initial thought was to suspend you for two weeks, but because you were thoughtful and contrite enough to come into the locker room and apologize, I am going to reduce it to one week. Therefore, I'm asking you to take a week off, and rejoin the game whenever you are ready after next Wednesday, April 10.

I have cut and pasted below the email message I sent out on May 11, 2011, after the last incident. You, along with everyone else, received it, so you can assume that you, and everyone else, had been warned.

See you in a week.

RICHIE

This may have prevented another fight, but four months later I was still concerned about the physical play on the part of these two.

I therefore sent one of those "eldering" emails I mentioned in the previous chapter to both the guy who threw the punch and the guy who received it. Here is what I wrote:

> I'd also like to ask the two of you to try to cut back on squabbling and arguing, and to be careful about how physically you play. I've had various complaints from more than one geezer, and my own observation is that the frequency and level of disputes increases when either of you is in the game. I, of course, want to keep the game as friendly as possible, and as injury-free as possible. Thanks for keeping this in mind.
>
> RICHIE

I shared this email with a few of the geezers. One responded in the following way: "AND that is why you are the Commissioner... nicely put... For 30 years I have waited for your book on bb demeanor and your demeanor in life... parallels and differences." Now, six or seven years later, the book you are reading is a belated effort to respond (in part) to his request.

There was a fourth physical confrontation, but I was not there and thus this is second-hand. In the mid- to late-1990s, before the Spears YMCA was built, there was a Y guy who played so aggressively that one of the geezers began to refer to him as Biff. One day, Biff threw an elbow at one of our bigger and stronger players, who then took a swing at Biff (and connected). The two of them apparently worked it out that day. However, Biff continued to play so aggressively that two geezers complained to the person who was running the facility, and he applied the standard penalty used by the YMCA—Biff was suspended for a month.

We have had no fights since 2013.

OFF THE COURT

THERE IS SOME banter on the court during games (though not a lot of trash talking), some brief conversations before and between games, and actual discussions about injuries, vacations, restaurants, books, or any number of other topics in the locker room before and after we play. Basketball is a social game both on and off the court, and this banter, these conversations, and sometimes real discussions have very much contributed to the sense of community and to the game's longevity.

Some geezer dialogue takes place online. Periodically, I send emails to all of the geezers, reminding them when their annual (or semi-annual) payments are due, that the gym will be closed for certain holidays, or that we will not have a court because of summer camps, resurfacing the floors, or whatever. Sometimes I send injury reports—when someone gets hurt, the others want to know how that person is doing. Over the years, many players have sustained injuries, usually minor, but sometimes requiring them to see a doctor, a dentist, or to go to a hospital. Once, memorably, when a guy came down with a rebound and his knee gave out (bringing back memories to some of us of a long-ago injury to NFL quarterback Joe

Theismann), he was carried off the court on a stretcher, definitely a career-ending injury. Most of the emails that I send generate few or no responses, but some have led to spirited exchanges.

The "Black Friday" emails

CONSIDER THE FOLLOWING chain of 16 emails, elicited by what I thought was a routine injury report, but which led to many responses over a four-day period, some humorous, some serious, about my use of the word "black" in the email's title.

1 *My email labeled "Black Friday," Nov. 6, 2004*

Geezers,

Friday took its toll. Though it looked like Bob Williams only pulled a muscle or some such, he actually broke a bone in his left foot. Details still to be determined, but he's in a cast, on crutches, and, though not in great pain, trying to figure out the ramifications (e.g., his car is stick shift). Andy was last seen with ice on his ankle.

For me, it seemed like the week went on forever. Sorry it ended with two injuries.

RICHIE

2 *First responder, Odell, Nov. 8 2004*

Why was Friday "black"....is "black" an adjective for "bad"???????? I love the geezer game........WHITE..... ODELL

3 *Next, Frank, Nov. 8, 2004*

Amen my black brother. I suggest to the commish that since he integrated geezer nation he has the responsibility of diversity and sensitivity training. He is to be commended for integrating above the population norm. I suggest that you, me, and Cook wear all white Wednesday with red, black, and green wrist-bands.

4 *Then, me again, Nov. 9, 2004*

Geezers,

I stand corrected by the Reverend Brother Odell, and I think Brother Frank's idea is a good one. I suggest we begin by addressing the following question, which I've been pondering:

Barack Obama, the Senator-elect from Illinois, is the son of an African father and a white mother. He was raised for a number of years in Hawaii by his white grandparents, and he attended the island's most elite private school, Punahou. Is he black? Why or why not?

Perhaps we can discuss this at the foul line, while people are shooting foul shots (oh, wait a minute, we don't shoot foul shots).

RICHIE

5 *Odell, Nov. 9, 2004*

GUYS...LET IT GO..........LET'S PLAY GEEZER BASKETBALL............BY THE WAY CHARLIE... WHAT COLOR IS THE BASKETBALL???????

6 *Rob, Nov. 9, 2004*

And in the immortal words of Freud, who spent countless hours pondering the implications of things, "sometimes a cigar is just a cigar."

7   *Odell, Nov. 9, 2010*

Rob, wasn't Freud....... "so smart that he lost his mind"..
.... "PSYCHO" or "PSYCHOPATHIC = engaging in amoral or antisocial acts without feeling remorse." Are you sure "sometimes a cigar is just a cigar", or a "BIG JOINT"...I MEAN THE GOOD STUFF...WITH A LITTLE "ANGELDUST" AS THE KICKER?????? REMEMBER....IT'S A REASON WHY THEY NAMED IT "ANGEL" DUST ———

8   *Frank, Nov. 9, 2004*

Look guys, I guess sarcasm does not come across well on a computer. Some of the responses show you get it, some do not. I respect each and every one of you. I am immensely thankful that you have allowed me the opportunity to be part of your group. So let us get over BLACK FRIDAY with no hard feelings and no hard fouls. I look forward to seeing you all tomorrow. Odell, I am still wearing WHITE and I want to be on the WHITE team.

9   *Odell, Nov. 9, 2004*

Dr. Hatchett........IT'S A GOOD THING THAT I WILL BE IN RALEIGH, NC ON WEDNESDAY.........MAYBE YOU WILL WIN A GAME OR TWO, MAYBE THREE......I ALSO AGREE MY FRIEND THAT ENOUGH IS ENOUGH...AND I ALSO WANT TO BE ON THE WHITE TEAM...YOU CAN'T BLAME ME....WHEN I LOOKED AT MR. WEBSTER'S DEFINITION OF (black and white).

   BLACK="(a)HARMFUL, EVIL, OR WICKED: A BLACK HEART (b)indicating censure, disgrace, etc.: a black mark on one's record (c)the color opposite to white."

WHITE= (a) AUSPICIOUS; FORTUNATE, MORALLY PURE; INNOCENT. (b) Lacking malice; harmless (c) the color opposite to black."

Wow .... ODELL

10 *Danny, Nov. 9, 2004*

Guys - thanks for the entertainment- I am at a Hilton in Chicago and it is boring!

I am going to miss Frank in white but I will wear gray on polka dot Friday! I actually like and RESPECT the geezers that wear black every day (I can only imagine how they describe the geezer game to others). I am only about 50/50 on the guys that wear white!

11 *Bob, Nov. 9, 2004*

Guys,

I am continually amazed by how pervasive racism is in our culture. Embedded in our language, most of our institutions, etc.

While our game is mostly about exercise, play and recreation, we do play on an educational institution.

Odell, thanks for raising the issue and making each of us more aware.

BOB

p.s. Getting back to basketball is easier for some than others of us.

12 *Claire, Nov. 9, 2004*

First, greetings to all from DC.

Second, to those who were injured on the sad Friday, I hope you heal well and quickly. Unfortunately, I know broken bones do not get hurried, so Bob Williams, I guess you will be out for a while. Sorry!

Third, the discussion has been interesting to read from this distance. Bob Williams, as we at Guilford say, "speaks my mind". Enjoy the basketball—no injuries, and cheers for pointing things out and kicking them around (maybe I should say passing them around).

CLAIRE

13 *Richard, Nov. 9, 2004*

Guys.... errr... Folks (don't forget sexism)...

14 *Lyn, Nov. 10, 2004*

Odell,

I have mixed emotions about the Commish's comments about "black" Friday.

Being half-Black[1], I am outraged on one hand—and ashamed on the other, by such a callous comment.

Always one to make peace, I will play for either team today—white or black. However, I only want to play on the offense.

LYN

15 *Ron, Nov. 10, 2004*

I have yet to comment on the current discussions running across the internet but I have found it fascinating and good fodder for the book I am writing.

---

1. Lyn revealed the next time he played that his mother's maiden name was Black.

The book is tentatively titled "Bald Like Me." Little has anyone known that I have disguised myself as a tall yet aging ball player who is follicly challenged with at least one bad knee, all to fit in with group of other aging men with varying degrees of hairlines, who feel a deep need to, dare I say,... sweat. In reality, I am 5'3" with a full head of hair, a graying beard, and a deadly 2-handed jump shot. Please keep it up. I have much yet to write and I have only gotten through the dedication to Wineburg part.

16 *Craig, Nov. 10, 2004: "Enough Black v. White!"*

I hate to have to come off the temporary D.L. to enter into this argument, but you all have left me no choice. I don't see the world in black or white. I don't see it as male or female. Those groups have been battling for years about who is and who isn't discriminating or being discriminated against. As far as I am concerned, the only group of people who have a right to complain about the way they have been portrayed are.... West Virginians. Yes, that's right. For years they have put up with being stereotyped as corn-cob pipe smoking, illiterate hillbillies.

Why, only this morning I heard on the radio "Why was the toothbrush invented in West Virginia?" The answer: "Because if was invented in any other state, they would have called it a teethbrush." Now THAT'S WHAT I'M TALKIN ABOUT. People definitely should not repeat jokes like that.

Social Capital

WHEN PEOPLE PLAY ball together three times a week, for years and years, it is not surprising that when life's various necessities arise, they sometimes turn to their teammates, at times for services, and at times for recommendations or advice. A mortgage? A foot doctor? Who's a good cardiologist, or who should I see to check out my ailing knee?

What we generally think of as "networking," French sociologist Pierre Bourdieu called "social capital." By this fancy term he meant the benefits that can accrue from such contacts, and he wanted to contrast it with economic capital (money itself) and cultural capital (knowledge and skills). Bourdieu and many other sociologists have shown that those from the privileged classes not only have more economic capital, and more cultural capital, but they also have more social capital than those from the lower classes. If Bourdieu were analyzing our game (hard to imagine), he would not fail to notice that most of the players are well-educated professionals—we have some doctors, professors, engineers, and owners of local businesses (in a few cases, owners or presidents of businesses that employ hundreds of people and do business regionally or nationally). Bourdieu might or might not notice, but I have, that we have had no lawyers in the game—this, I have said only half-jokingly, might have contributed to our longevity.[2]

Bourdieu would observe that if I (a professor) want to redo my mortgage, or need a recommendation for a doctor who is really good (sports injury? prostate? you name it), one of my hoop buddies is likely to be helpful, or have contacts who might be helpful. By playing in the game, I have accrued social capital. Not surprisingly, therefore, over the years, many geezers have made visits to the foot doctor who plays in the game (and consulted with him in the locker room), a number have arranged for mortgages and remortgages by the mortgage banker in the game, some have asked for, and gotten, recommendations about long-term life insurance from one of the players who owned an insurance agency, and some have asked for, and received, editorial help as they have worked on articles or books

2. Technically we have had two lawyers play, one as a guest and another as a short-term participant until he accepted an out-of-town job. Neither achieved geezer status.

(including me, on this book). One of our many unwritten rules is that such consultations should take place in the locker room, but not on the court, especially during games.

Our game is not unusual in this respect. All groups are likely to provide the opportunity for participants to accrue social capital. The urologist I go to tells me that he took up hockey at the age of 35, that he now plays one night a week with a bunch of guys he otherwise would never have met, and that half of the men on his team are now his patients.

Over the years, therefore, the geezers have come to know one another on the court, but also off the court. They do business with each other, seek advice from one another, and some socialize. Some play golf together on non-basketball days.

People Die

SOME OF THOSE who have played in the geezer game have died, though thankfully not on the court. So, too, have geezers lost family members—numerous parents, a wife, and in one case, a daughter. The geezers have stepped up when these deaths have occurred. When the daughter of one of our players died in 2013, we quickly raised $300 to contribute to the organization designated in the obituary (the Gateway Education Center). When the wife of one of the geezers died in in 2017, a crew of 8-10 of the geezers drove to nearby Kernersville, NC, to attend the funeral. These off-court gestures have meant a lot to those dealing with death.

The Geezers Go to the Ballpark

WE ALSO HAVE had many social gatherings. For example, the geezers have gone, en masse, to watch Guilford's men's and women's basketball teams play, to watch the daughters of one of the guys play in a high school basketball tournament, and to a batting cage to settle a bet over whether one of the geezers, Bob Wineburg, a former college baseball player, could still, at the age of 64, hit a baseball coming at him at 90 miles per hour (he could). These excursions typically were followed by those in attendance going somewhere to drink beer.

One memorable occasion took us to the local minor league ballpark to see the Class A Greensboro Grasshoppers. In 2007, Danny McCoy, who at the time was working for MetLife, invited all the geezers to attend a game at the new ballpark. MetLife had a "luxury box" in the second deck above the first base line where one could sit on comfortable furniture, watch the game, and be served beer and sandwiches. Danny not only reserved the box for the geezers, but he arranged with the ballpark's powers that be for me (as Commissioner of the geezer game) to throw out the first pitch. That morning, I practiced in the street in front of my house with Bob Wineburg, my next-door neighbor. After trying many options, I decided to go with a Luis (Look Back at the Center Field Wall) Tiant delivery, and to throw a curve ball. I was one of three people throwing out "first pitches." The other two were six years old and ten years old (I was 62). Mine was the only one of the three pitches that made it to the plate without bouncing, though it was low and outside. When I made it up to the luxury box to join the other geezers, Frank Hatchett (an all-state guard when he played for the Greensboro Day School) raised his fist and said "Luis Tiant!"

Big-Number Birthdays

WE ALSO HAVE celebrated various big-number birthdays (those divisible by 5, or 10, or 25) by reserving a room at a restaurant or bar and meeting for beer, sometimes for dinner as well as beer. These have been spirited events, especially when Andy Casper, one of the (younger) geezers who grew up not only playing football, baseball, and basketball, but also the accordion, brought his instrument with him and part of the "program" consisted of him leading us in song (the highlight, a spirited rendition of "Country Roads," dedicated to Danny McCoy, a native of West Virginia—and proud of it). At some of these events, I have used a PowerPoint Presentation to give joke awards.

When I turned 70, in 2015, the geezers insisted that we go out for beer to celebrate my hitting such a momentous non-prime number. Reluctantly, I agreed, assuming that maybe someone would take over my role and be the emcee, giving me and others grief, with the kinds of fake awards that I often included. When Lisa and I got there, I was surprised to see a much bigger crew than usually attended these events, including many long-retired geezers who had not played in the game for years, even decades. When the program began, various guys spoke about the game, and my leadership, in very nice ways (it was not in any sense a roast). And then, much to my surprise, one of them announced that they had arranged to name one of the courts in Ragan-Brown after me and showed me a mock-up of what the court would look like. A sub-group of geezers had approached administrators at the college about this (including Jon, the VP), were told it could actually happen if some amount of money was raised. It was only when writing this account, four years after the event, that it occurred to me to ask how much it took. Apparently in an exploratory meeting at the Mexican restaurant across the street from the college, each of five or six geezers on the "planning team" was challenged by Jon to put up $500 toward the needed fund-raising goal, which was not specified. They all agreed to pony up that amount (how about that!) and then some effort was made to raise additional money from other geezers. My guess is that between $3,000 and $10,000 was raised (and my wife tells me that she heard that the actual amount was $7,000).

Just as he had arranged for the clock and the plaque that the geezers had purchased to be mounted on the wall a few years earlier, Jon arranged for my name to be applied to the court, just like Mike Krzyzewski's at Duke.[3] A few weeks later, there it was (it says, "Richie's Court: Richie 'The Commish' Zweigenhaft").

As also noted above, Jon lost his job a month or so later, without warning, escorted off campus with his personal effects—gone but not forgotten, neither seen nor heard from since. The geezers had mixed feelings, depending in part on whether they had to cover, or be covered by, him. There was, however, consensus on one thing: as one geezer put it, "Glad we got Richie's name on the court before Jon's departure."

In June 2016, Steve Schlehuser, the oldest guy in the game, celebrated his 75th birthday. We generally referred to him as "Old Steve" until he turned 65 in 2006, at which point, as a sign of respect, we began to call him "Steve the Elder." Five years later, when he turned 70, we began to call him "Steve the Really Elder." At a celebration we had for his 75th birthday, I suggested that we should call him "Steve the Really, Really Elder," and that when he got to be 80 we should call him "Steve the Ancient." For that 75th birthday celebration, we rented a back room at a restaurant, invited wives and partners, drank beer, listened to and sang along with music on the accordion by Andy Casper, and had a PowerPoint-guided "program," complete with awards (e.g., Rookie of the Year, shared by Todd Clark and Tim Murphy, Most Improved Player, won by Mark Harris, Best Comeback from Surgery, shared by Andy Casper and Rob Luisana, Most Banked in Threes, won—no contest—by Thom Espinola, and the Stephen Curry Award, won by Frank Hatchett). A good time was had by all.

Trump

A FEW MONTHS later, Trump was elected. We have not had a celebratory all-geezer gathering, birthday or otherwise, since that

---

3. I have joked many times that this is the only thing Coach K and I have in common.

election. I have a very clear memory of eating lunch with a few geezers one Friday (a subgroup of us often have lunch together after the games on Friday). It was March 2016, a week or so before the North Carolina primary, and we were eating at a Mexican restaurant across the street from the college. One of the guys who was there (an outspoken liberal) asked another (an outspoken conservative) if he was going to vote for Trump. The conservative said that Trump was not his first choice, "but," he went on to say, "I can live with Trump."

I grew up in a Jewish family, and my undergraduate honors thesis was a psychological analysis of Hitler's personality. In doing the research for the thesis, in discussions with my thesis advisor (an eminent Russian historian, also Jewish), and in the years since, I have read about, and thought about, how Hitler had enough popular support to become Chancellor of Germany in 1933. Sitting there in the Mexican restaurant, I had a very eerie feeling. I could not shake this image that we were sitting in a restaurant in Germany in January 1933 (probably not a Mexican restaurant), and this friendly, educated, and good-natured guy that I play basketball with (in Germany in 1933 we more likely would have been playing soccer), might have said, casually, that Hitler wasn't his first choice, but he could live with him.

Trump won the North Carolina primary, edging out Ted Cruz, 40% to 37%. As the 2016 election approached, and Trump had become the Republican nominee, it was clear that some of those in the geezer game were going to vote for him, and a few were outspoken Trump supporters. Two of the geezers, memorably (to me), made clear that they thought that both Donald Trump and Hillary Clinton were awful and that it wouldn't matter which was elected. At least one geezer proudly informed the others of us that he had been driving Trump voters to the polls for early voting and planned to do so on election day. When Trump was elected, I was devastated, and I knew that some of the Trump-supporting geezers were celebrating (they were, perhaps, every bit as happy as I had been when Obama was elected). The next day was Wednesday, a basketball day, but I had no classes, and no office hours, and no (real) committee meetings, so I stayed home. I did not want to see anyone, especially those who had happily voted for Trump.

For the most part, Trump's election has not affected the game. We still play three days a week, and I no longer think to myself, every time I see those who voted for Trump, "How could that guy have supported such a crude, narcissistic, misogynistic, racist, wanna-be dictator?" Nor have I asked any of them if they still support him, or if they will vote for him again in 2020. As I have indicated, one of my guiding principles when it comes to the geezer game is to try to minimize arguments. I will admit that if I were a more tolerant person perhaps I'd be willing, perhaps even eager, to talk about these profound differences in world-view over a beer with these guys, but I'm not. So far, at least, I have not been willing to resume my role as the social chairman who arranges geezer-inclusive celebrations for big birthdays. Maybe I will once again want to enjoy everyone's company in that way. Meanwhile, the game goes on, having survived differences among the players about Ronald Reagan, the two Bushes, Bill Clinton, and Barack Obama. Maybe the game (and the country) will survive Trump.

SOME REASONS FOR THE GAME'S LONGEVITY

IT IS IMPOSSIBLE, of course, to know why the game has lasted as long as it has. Many factors have been at play, and I am sure it is the confluence of these, plus many I am not aware of, along with a dollop (or maybe more) of good luck. The ones that come to mind are the following:

1   Good guiding principles, accepted by those who play. Among these are the ones I listed at the end of the opening chapter: 1) everyone plays an equal amount; 2) injuries and arguments are to be minimized; and 3) friendship first.

2   What I have called "participatory autocracy," in which everyone's voice is heard but ultimately I have made a decision (without actual votes almost all of the time and without the need for consensus). This may not be as unQuakerly as it sounds. Even in a Quakeresque setting such as the college where I teach, there are times when consensus has not been reached but a decision must be made (deadlines, for example, require someone, often the President, sometimes the Board, to make a choice to go one way or another).

3   Back in 2003, negotiating a good, long-term, working agreement with the college to rent a court three times a week. Here, again, the wise decision of Guilford's former President, Kent Chabotar, to allow the nonGuilfordians to continue to play in the Guilford gym, should be applauded.

4   The willingness to adjust, as is most apparent in the many rule changes we have enacted over time—especially adding the three-point shot, trying Half Court Mondays for a year or two, and the subsequent switch to half court all the time.

5   Keeping the game competitive but not allowing it to become too aggressive. Keeping it competitive has included efforts to make teams that are well-matched, so that the games will be close. Keeping it from getting too competitive has been a bigger challenge. As I have indicated, we have had a few physical confrontations but, fortunately, only a few.

6   Having a woman in the game. From the time we started playing back in 1976 in the Crackerbox, until she retired from teaching at Guilford in 2013, Claire Morse, my colleague in the psychology department, was a regular participant. At times, other women have played, but none as frequently or for as many years as Claire. When she and her husband lived in El Salvador in the early 1970s, she practiced with the women's national team. Although she was never a dominant player in our game, and typically was not a high scorer, she might have one of the highest "career" shooting percentages of anyone who has played. Moreover, and this is the point I want to make here, the fact that we usually had a woman on the court helped us establish values that have contributed to the game's longevity. That is to say, I believe our game has been less aggressive than it might have been and has had less stereotypical macho behavior (fights? arguments? trash talking?) because on most

days there was a female presence—and especially because it was Claire, who is consistently good-natured, fair, and cares about people's feelings.

7   Having a core of players who have been around for a long time. This includes academics with tenure (because of tenure, they were not going to lose their teaching jobs unless they committed what used to be called "moral turpitude") but also Greensboro residents who did not change jobs a lot, or, if they did change jobs, were still able to play basketball a few times a week in the middle of the day. Also: we have been fortunate to have doctors (especially when there were injuries) and, I suspect, fortunate not to have lawyers.

Perhaps these things contributed to the longevity of the game, and perhaps they can provide some guidance for others hoping to keep their pickup basketball games going. Who knows, maybe some of these factors, and some of the ideas I have shared in this quirky little account might help in non-basketball settings, as people try to keep other games going, or, in work settings, as they try to keep everyone involved and arguments and fights to a minimum. Friendship first. Respect the call. You don't stop playing because you grow old; you grow old because you stop playing.

APPENDICES

Appendix 1. My June 2003 Email to the Geezers

OKAY, GEEZERS, listen up (as my junior high school basketball coach used to say). Better yet, print this out so you can study it carefully, for there are decisions to be made.

As I mentioned in my email yesterday, I met with Brian Wenger, the Director of the athletic facility at the college. Guilford now has a system whereby we can continue to use the gym for geezer basketball. Basically, the college has rental agreements for its various facilities, and we can arrange to rent the basketball court for the days we want it. The regular fee for the Ragan-Brown Field House is $45/hour, but special discount rates (40% off) are provided for coaches and distinguished professors of psychology. This means we can rent the gym for $27 an hour. Brian assured me that we could reserve the court for an hour (say, noon to 1) but we could come earlier and stay later most of the time, and he would only charge us for the one hour. He'd like us to try to be done by 1:15 or 1:30 at the latest, so we probably will need to start by 11:30. We would reserve the court semester by semester, and either pay at the outset for the whole semester or pay by the month.

If we were to stay with our three day a week schedule, three hours a week over a 17-week semester at $27 an hour means a cost of $1377. If we were to switch to two days a week, it would come to $918. First question for you to think about is what days we should reserve. I have three options for you to consider: the traditional Monday, Wednesday, Friday; Tuesday and Thursday; or, option number 3, Tuesday, Thursday and Friday.

Second question is whether you're willing to pony up an initial fee that would put your name on the list to gain access to the gym. Brian plans to have that list at the front desk, and only people on the list will be allowed downstairs during the time we've rented the gym. Others who have legitimate access to the facility, such as students, staff and other faculty, will be directed to the upstairs gym during the time we've rented the field house. Those without legitimate access to the facility will not be allowed in. At some point "membership" cards may be issued, but it's not clear when that will happen. There is no plan to provide towels, which Brian tells me seem to disappear at alarming rates, so the bring your own towel policy will remain in effect.

The current, working, geezer list (see below) has about 30 names on it, but some of the people on the list have not been seen for a while. How much we end up paying will in part be determined by the number of geezers who sign on. For the time being, I'm suggesting an initial payment of $150 per person. If 15 people sign on, that's $2250, which covers our monthly fees well beyond December, and means I don't have to keep asking for smaller amounts (I'm not asking Guilford faculty to pay this fee, since use of the gym is one of the many, many benefits for employees here at Guilford College). As for "membership," I'm planning to start with the geezer email list and see how many sign on. We'll then decide if we want or need more people. My sense is that we'll have enough.

I'm sure that there will be decisions to make along the way about membership and other matters. My plan is to make these decisions myself, unless I want or need help. If I do, then I will draw on a Guilford College Interdisciplinary Basketball-Playing Faculty Kitchen Cabinet consisting of Thom Espinola (physics), Claire Morse (psychology) and Bob Williams (economics). In addition, I'm assuming that at times, I'll poll all paying members (to decide, for example, whether to include a new person in the game, or, just to come up with a wild example, whether to ban someone who makes the mistake of starting a fight or throwing the ball in someone's face).

Brian also said we would either need a liability policy of $1 million, or we would each need to sign a form waiving liability. I told him the latter seemed to make more sense to me, and I have copies of the form each of you will need to sign.

Okay, so here's what you need to do. First, let me know what your preferences are for game days (this you could do by email). Second, send a check made out to me for $150 (Richie Zweigenhaft, Psychology Dept., Guilford College, Greensboro, NC 27410). When I get your check, I'll either send you a copy of the waiver form through the mail, or I'll slip one to you in the locker room, though let me stress that I don't really want to conduct the business of this operation in the locker room or on the court. Brian would like to move to this system in July, perhaps before they spend a few weeks working on the floor, but maybe after they have done the floor.

Here's the working list of geezers, based on the list I sent Brian Wenger a few months back, and the email list I'm currently using (note that I have emails for most, but not all of the people on the list). If you know of regular players who are not on the list and you think they should be, let me know.

Brian Allen	Dan Lenze
Mike Brown	Greg Mayer
Craig Chappelow	Danny McCoy
Odell Cleveland	Claire Morse
Nathan Cook	Robert Pearse
George Cox	David Ratclifte
Thom Espinola	Steve Reid
Frank Hatchett	Charlie Richmond
Rusty Hoffman	Darryl Rollandelli
Ron Irons	Steve Schlehuser
Charlie Johnson	Jerrold Wheeler
Lyn Keller	Bob Williams
Steve Lemberg	Bob Wineburg
Mark Lewis	Richie Zweigenhaft
Rob Luisana	

Appendix 2. Articles About the Geezer Game and Dead Men Dribbling

Appendix 2A. "Guilford's Noontime Basketball" by Claire Morse[1]

"LET'S GO, IT'S TIME for the Committee Meeting." The meeting is indicated on the Correspondence Center schedule forms of some of us, and the admonition might be heard Monday, Wednesday, or Friday in several faculty offices. This committee meets more often than others—and it is much more enjoyable, too. On our way over to the gym, Richie and I are as likely to be discussing teaching or Guilford business as anything else. We stop only on entering our separate locker rooms. As basketballs bounce on the wooden Alumni Gym floor, the noises of warming up are mixed with greetings, heckling and business. Not just any business, more Guilford College business. After all, lots of the players are Guilford faculty or staff. Others are current Guilford students, some are graduates. Yet others are members of the Y. This committee has met faithfully at noontime on Monday, Wednesday and Friday for the last eight years. Members may serve repeated terms, and several leaves of absence have been granted. Membership is open, requiring only that one enjoy playing basketball. Skills are desirable, but not mandatory. Student eligibility also is unlimited by years or academic standing. Attendance is not officially recorded, although infrequent attendance will almost certainly be noted, and heckling may result. Tardiness is often costly—if there is not an odd number of players, or the game has already begun, the late player will probably have to wait to play. The character of this game might be captured by noting the number of players who do not know the score at any time, and by the perhaps even larger number who do not remember who won the previous meeting day (or perhaps even later that afternoon).

1. Morse, Claire. 1985. "The Committee Meeting: Guilford's Noontime Basketball." *Guilford Review* 22(Fall):19; see Appendix 2A.

The scheduled meeting time is 12:00. Actually, we usually begin playing after 12:15. It is difficult to break up the business meetings going on during the warm-up period. It is far more arduous to make up teams. Although only a few players are willing to suggest teams, all have an interest in establishing the team membership. We play competitively, and evenly matched teams make the games more interesting. Moreover, there are some match-ups to be avoided as too likely to produce dispute. Friction between players diminishes the enjoyment—and the playing time—for everyone. Even though people are reluctant to suggest teams, if someone doesn't do so, most will urge that we get started. Someone, or several people, will eventually designate the "skins" and "shirts." In spite of numerous jokes and offers, I have always been a "shirt." There may be some joking remarks about unfair teams, but they never last long.

The unwritten rules of this game commit us to seeing that everyone who comes gets a chance to play. We will divide into two games rather than requiring that a group of players wait for winners of the first game. Our game has grown over the years so that having two games is not unusual now, and having available both the Alumni Gym court and a court in the new field house is a wonderful luxury. This year we have frequently had enough for two full-court, four-on-four games, and even two five-on-five games—20 players—a few times. These crowds represent steady growth from the days when three-on-three was the typical committee meeting.

I am fairly sure that my presence has raised a few (male) eyebrows. I am the only woman who has played regularly. Sometimes a woman student or a couple of women from the basketball team have joined our game, but this has been rare. And one noon we played against the Guilford women's team. Apparently Coach Currie wanted the women to see how aggressively the game can be played. Being the only woman has always been interesting. Initially I was quite nervous, both about how well I could play and whether the men would include me in the game when I was on the court. That feeling diminished as I had a few successful games, and I acquired a certain measure of longevity, not to mention seniority. (By now, at 42, I am one of the oldest players). I think that the men make some adjustments to the presence of a woman. For example, I think there is hesitation on the part of new players about what sort of language is acceptable in this game. Some players never seem to express emotional responses in "four letter words," and some men have apologized to me for their word choice; however, since I use some foul words myself, I think that at least frees most of the men from the injunction prohibiting cursing around women and permits a release of frustration with a loud expletive on the part of other players, I am also not the only one who groans or chides myself for a missed shot or poor play. I do shout in unhappiness more than most, and was warned before going to U Mass on a study leave three years ago not to do that there. I did, and again found that there were a few others who also did. But few.

Physical contact and fouling can lead to conflict in any pickup game, and they sometimes do at the Committee Meeting. We each call fouls committed against us, and frequently we call those we commit on another player. I sometimes sense that my male opponents will call fouls against themselves when those infractions are committed on me which they would not call if their opponent were another male. And sometimes men apologize to me for incidental contact. But then, I apologize to them for the same sort of thing. Perhaps the reciprocity which I value—I'll try to call my fouls fairly and I will expect you to do likewise—is best established that way. It seems a generally shared attitude during our meetings. I do despise losing the ball to superior male upper body muscle strength, but it happens and seems inevitable. I do not mind being sent flying by some simple collision with a heavier player since I view that as part of playing the game, and have never sensed that any of the other players were malicious or intent on causing injury. Unaware of other players, perhaps, but not mean.

I'd like to know more about what the game has meant to other players. For me it has provided wonderful exercise with a group of people including some whom I would otherwise not know or spend time with. These men are comrades of a special sort, and our shared play can certainly lead me to respect and enjoy them from the perspective of a woman who has been allowed to participate simply as another player in a game we all enjoy. The game has provided me the basis for further appreciation of several members of the Guilford College community who are fun to play ball with, and who bring basketball talents one might not have expected from being at other committee meetings together. The contact with students has also been of a special sort. Student players have been numerous over the years, if not quite as regular as others. The chance to play with or against a student who is or has been in one of my classes is a special opportunity to see him (rarely her) moving fast, shooting well, and beating a professor to a rebound. There is humbling, there is winning, there is joking. I've not sensed gloating or belittling. I know that students know about the noontime game, and they must therefore realize that a group of men and women, from high school to "middle age," can play decent basketball and take great delight in it. After all the faculty members of the Committee Meeting have always played better than .500 ball in the intramural league.

The Committee Meeting continues, we welcome new players, and anticipate steady growth in numbers. Perhaps a new field house?

Appendix 2B. "Order on the Court: A Lesson in Leadership" by Craig Chappelow[2]

IN THESE DAYS of jargon-filled mission statements, it is refreshing to find an example of a leader walking the talk. I am lucky that I get to see an example of this mission clarity every week. All I have to do is pick up my sneakers and head out of the office at lunchtime. At the Guilford College YMCA in my hometown of Greensboro, North Carolina, there is a group of people who spend the lunch hour playing in a pickup basketball game. Nothing particularly unusual about that—except that this lunch game started twenty-four years ago and is still going strong. Group members have come and gone over the years, but a steady core of banged-up, liniment-covered hasbeens continue to strap on their high-tops and go at it as if the NBA title were at stake. For the thirty or so men and women who play regularly, it is the highlight of the week. Our mission statement, if we had one, would be something like this: "Get exercise."

The group is a hodgepodge of former jocks and nonathletes from all professions. Last week my teammates consisted of an engineer, a podiatrist, an artist, and a guy who collects tractors. All of us have one thing in common. We depend on being able to show up, get into a game quickly, get some exercise, take a shower, and get back to work before anyone notices we were gone.

Keeper of the Flame

HOW IS IT that this particular game has endured for twenty-four years? A great deal of the credit must go to the leader, Richie Zweigenhaft. It is easy to overlook Richie because he is usually the smallest player on the court. With his oversized safety goggles,

2. Chappelow, Craig. 2000. "Order on the Court: A Lesson in Leadership." *Leadership in Action* 20(5):13-14.

headband, long shorts, high socks, and bushy beard, he looks more like a psychology professor than like a ballplayer. That's probably because he is a psychology professor—more Carl Jung than Karl Malone. It was Richie who, together with a handful of other Guilford College faculty members, started this pickup game twenty-four years ago, and it is Richie who consistently walks the talk.

I have learned some important things about leadership from watching Richie. Most of these tips are things that I think any leader could apply to his or her work:

Be clear about your mission. The mission for our group is to get a workout. Everything else comes second. Years ago, Richie and the other charter members established a system of rotating players in and out of the games and across the courts to reduce the amount of time people have to wait to play. Even if you show up late, you will be rotated into a game within a few minutes.

Don't waste your team members' time. Everyone who plays in the noon league has a limited amount of time at lunch. That means that chitchat about last night's football game on TV or a discussion of departmental politics must wait. By modeling this kind of focus, Richie has transmitted this priority to the other players. He is a nice guy, but if you try to indulge in small talk with him between games, he'll politely shrug you off as he gets the next game under way. This is not out of rudeness but rather is in service to the mission. Another professor in Richie's department at Guilford College who is a regular lunch league player, Claire Morse, says Richie's off-court leadership behaviors are similar: "He is well prepared for his responsibilities and takes them seriously, but he finds ways to enjoy them too. He makes other people's lives better in the process."

Confront problems swiftly but selectively and calmly. The majority of the players in the noon league are middle-age folks well on the downhill side of their sports skills—if they had any such skills to begin with. There are enough spare tires on the court to outfit a tractor-trailer. Even so, the games can get highly competitive. When an argument breaks out between two players, Richie quietly changes the defensive assignments. This separates the two players and reduces the chance of further problems. Richie doesn't try to mediate between the players or reach a resolution. That would detract from the mission. Bob Wineburg, a professor of social work at the University of North Carolina at Greensboro and a longtime league member, describes Richie's problem-solving style this way: "He doesn't lecture; he makes strategic moves." In my thirteen years of playing in the league I have seen Richie annoyed, frustrated, and discouraged but never angry.

Seek fairness and balance. Everyone looks to Richie to divide the players into teams to get the games started—not because the rest of us can't but because Richie has an uncanny knack for setting up balanced teams. Dan McCoy, a mortgage banker and lunch league regular, points out that "Richie would enjoy nothing more than a three-game split with the scores 15 to 13. As some of us approach our fifth decade, if not for Richie's influence on the noon game we would be forced to abandon the game we love."

Lead by example. Ralph Waldo Emerson is credited with saying, "What you do speaks so loudly that I cannot hear what you say." Richie doesn't say much, but his actions say a great deal. If we have to stop a competitive game and send two players to the next court to fill out teams to start a second game, Richie will go. He would rather pass the ball than shoot—although he shoots well. Most of all he doesn't do anything that doesn't serve the mission of the group.

Appendix 2C. "Men Score at Senior Games" by Rob Luisana[3]

WHILE WE ENTERED the Senior Game basketball game competition under the team name, Dead Men Dribbling, we were actually Geezer basketball players. That is, the group of older basketball players who had migrated to Guilford College to play in the lunch time basketball games that were held there, three days a week.

For myself and many of the other players, it had been a long road to Geezer basketball, covering basketball courts from what was called the Rocket ship park on Market Street in the 70's, to the games outdoors at Lake Daniels Park, to the First Baptist Church, to the small outdoor court at College Park, to the Central YMCA, to Sportime and finally to the Guilford College Gym. Most players are over 40, a few over 55, the qualifying age to play in the North Carolina Senior Games.

When Bob Wineburg, one of the Geezer basketball players, told several of us Geezers that he had been diagnosed with cancer, all of us were amazed at the courage and humor with which he approached the disease. I had played basketball with and against Bob for years at Guilford College, and we'd known one another as neighbors in the Aycock neighborhood before that. When he told me about his diagnosis of cancer, I tried to think of ways to cheer him, and the one thing that I knew would get him excited was the idea of competition.

After his surgery, I visited with him while he was recovering. We walked slowly around his block and talked about playing basketball in the Senior Games. In spite of his pain, he was clearly excited about the idea.

I had thought about playing in the Senior Games before Bob's illness pushed me to sign up. Part of the reason to play was to fight back against getting older. I was 56, not only receiving literature from

3. Luisana, Rob. 2006. "Men Score at Senior Games." *News & Record*, January 16, 10–12.

AARP, but old enough to join. Turning 30, 40 and 50 hadn't fazed me; somehow, 55 was more of a milestone. Maybe playing in a basketball tournament was one way to fight the fact that I was getting older.

Certainly there aren't many 55-and-older ball players left—injuries and just plain wear and tear take a toll. Many of my friends quit playing basketball saying, "I just got tired of hurting all the time." Over the past 20 years, I had racked up an assortment of injuries. Broken foot, which put me on crutches for a month. Broken nose, bad enough to have it reset. My wife, Karen, had pushed hard for getting the nose reset. Finally, a compartment injury to my left calf. My list of injuries is not unusual for someone who plays competitive basketball for 40 years. Many Geezer players list a similar assortment of injuries.

When we played against each other, Wineburg complained often and loudly about the way I played, claiming that I was fouling or going over his back to get to the ball or generally being too competitive. But he wanted to win every basketball game we played and was probably the most competitive of all of us Geezers. With Wineberg and myself, we were still at least 3 players short of a team. The Senior Games are half-court, three-on-three and we needed at least two substitutes.

We were desperate for a big man. I knew, I didn't want to be the designated big man, since I'm 6'1" and weigh 185 pounds. Unfortunately there was no big man around. Knees and other body parts essential to playing basketball begin to wear out after 30 and that is especially true for bigger players.

We recruited the best three over-55 Geezers available. Next on board was Richie Zweigenhaft, all 5-foot-7 and 130 pounds. Smart player, unselfish, good shooter and passer and already established as the preeminent Geezer leader. Not because he was the best player, but because he was always trying to do what was right. He was allowed to pick the teams and did so fairly. To promote sportsmanship and to make everyone feel good, he even admonished us to no longer refer to our oldest player as "old Steve" but as "Steve the Elder." He was going to be a member of the team as much for his ability to stay level-headed as for his basketball skills.

Our next recruit was Lynn Keller, a strong player. Best one-on-one player we had. Excellent shooter from 15 feet to 18 feet and able to drive to the basket, take a foul and still make the shot; rebounded well for his size, 5 foot 10, and always played hard. He packed the most immaculate gym bag I had ever seen.

Our final player was Charlie Johnson, who at 6-foot-1 is an excellent shooter and a smart player. He created shots for himself by constant movement. Of the five of us, Charlie was the only local boy. He played high school basketball at Southeast High in the 60's. Charlie played to win and often got into arguments over his willingness to foul rather than to give up an easy shot. His size and toughness would help us on the boards and offset some of my weaknesses.

When it became known that we would play in the Senior Games some Geezer players predicted how we would do. Probably the most telling scouting report came from Danny McCoy, who wrote in an email analysis of the team: "Strong offense, limited rebounding, really strong on rule interpretation."

I had given little thought to how well we would fit together as teammates, assuming five senior citizens could coexist and play together without a problem. But one day, after we finished playing and showering, I heard loud, angry noises coming from the locker room.

I walked out to find teammates Charlie Johnson and Bob Wineburg screaming at one another, faces 10 inches apart. The source of the argument was, incredibly, George Bush's speech on Social Security and tax policy. This was new ground for me. In 40-plus years of playing basketball, I heard and witnessed plenty of locker room arguments, along with a few fights, all of which involved either a girl or another player's unwillingness to share the basketball. This was the first time I'd seen two basketball players preparing to come to blows over tax policy.

I walked into the locker room and looked at Bob Williams, who was laughing. I said, "Well, do you think the team is going to have chemistry problems?" He responded, "Look at the players on the team and tell me how you're not going to have problems." The Senior Games were uncharted territory for all of us.

The guidelines to participate in the Games required that we play several practice games with a referee and under the official Senior Games rules. Our first scrimmage game was set against some of the younger Geezer players who had not yet reached the qualifying age-55 mark. Despite not having Charlie Johnson, who was injured, and being at a clear height disadvantage, we won two out of three games.

The second series of practice games came against the 60–65 age team from Winston-Salem. The games were competitive, and the Winston-Salem team would go on to win the State in their division. We won all 3 games and began to actually think we would be a factor when we went to Greenville in October.

We arrived at the ECU student center for the Saturday morning opening ceremonies along with teams from across North Carolina. The competition was divided into age brackets for men's and women's teams. The youngest bracket was ages 55-59. There would be 16 men's teams and eight women's teams in this age group. The number of teams dropped with each bracket. Twelve teams competed in the 60-65 men's bracket, three in the women's group. The oldest team from Orange County competed in the 80 and above men's division, the only team entered. Longevity has its rewards.

Our first game was against the Pitt County team. While we had the shortest team in the competition, they had the tallest. Despite the size disadvantage, we led for most of the first half and went into the halftime break down by only three points. We ended up losing by nine points.

We won the second game easily by 20 points. Lynn and Charlie led the scoring, but everyone played well.

The competition was divided into pools of four or five teams with the top two teams from each pool advancing to the quarterfinals.

Our third game against a team from Western Carolina would determine if we advanced.

The Western Carolina team was almost as big as the Pitt County team, definitely physical. The game was close with neither team able to generate more than a five-point lead. There was a great deal of shoving and fouling, much never called by the referees.

Our lack of size and bulk hurt us, as well as the fact that we couldn't stop their best player, who must have scored 75 percent of their points. The game ended with a three-point loss.

We wouldn't advance to play Sunday. Still, there was something worthwhile about being there. It was certainly inspiring to watch men and women 20 years older than us out on the basketball court continuing to compete.

POSTSCRIPT: Deadmen Dribbling returned to the Senior Games again this past October and with the addition of Tally Mitchell as a player and Frank Hatchett as coach managed to win two out of three games in their pool.

They're still looking for an over-55 post player.

Appendix 2D. "The Geezer Game and Dead Men Dribbling" by Richie Zweigenhaft [4]

I USED TO THINK that our mid-day geezer basketball game here at Guilford was unique. Three days a week, a bunch of us, now ranging in age from 40-65, play five-on-five full court basketball at Guilford College. The game began back in 1976, in the old gym (Alumni Gym), known then by all as "the crackerbox." For many years, we called the game "the committee meeting" so that when actual committees we were on tried to schedule meetings during our sacred basketball time, we'd say that we couldn't meet then because had another meeting scheduled.

Many who have played in our game through the years have retired or moved away, but here we are, 30 years later, still playing, three days a week, full court, most days in Ragan-Brown, but some days in Alumni Gym. The game, now known (affectionately, but also officially) as "the geezer game," consists of faculty, staff and a bunch of guys who used to be YMCA members when the college had an affiliation with the Y, and who now pay dues to rent the court three times a week (I used to be known as Rockaday Johnny, but now some call me "the commissioner"). Hung on the rafters are imaginary banners with the imaginary retired numbers of former participants, such as John "Radar" Stoneburner, Mel "Truck" Keiser, and Ken "Indiana Hook Shot" Schwab.

Our game probably is unique, in the same way that no two snowflakes, no two people, and no two pickup basketball games are exactly the same. But now that a subgroup of our geezer game has competed in a statewide three-on-three half court tournament at East Carolina University (ECU) that is part of something called "The Senior Games," I realize that there are geezers

4. Zweigenhaft, Richie. 2006. "The Geezer Game and Dead Men Dribbling." (http://class.guilford.edu/pages/modules/10000/depts/psychology/richie/bball.htm)

throughout North Carolina still putting up jumpers, 1950's-style hook shots, and occasional air balls.

Our team ("Dead Men Dribbling") was one of 16 teams entered in the 55-59-year-old bracket. I was surprised that there were so many teams at that advanced age (well, I'm closer to 62 than to 61, but I was "playing down"). I was even more surprised that there were 12 men's teams in the 60-64-year-old bracket, a bunch of teams in the 65-69-year-old bracket, some in the 70-74 and 74-79 year old brackets, and, get this, two teams in the over-80 bracket. There were also women's teams, ranging in age from 55 to 75. In short, for one autumn week-end the fancy new sports palace at ECU, clearly built to attract virile young college students, was filled with geezers who still play basketball.

So how'd we do? Well, in the first game we played a team from Pinehurst ("Pinehurst Hip and Knee Bobcats"), the first of three games we were to play against opponents who were bigger than we were at each position every minute of every game. Though we were smaller, we were also quicker, and we played well. In the last minute of the game, we lost the small lead we had been holding, but we then eked out a win on a shot with three seconds left by 59-year-old Lyn Keller. An hour later, in game two, against a team called "Hoopsters," from somewhere in North Carolina, but I'm not sure where, we jumped to a lead midway through the first half, which we kept, winning by 14 points. As time began to wind down in the second half, the Hoopsters began to foul us as soon as we passed the ball in, and we spent a lot of time at the foul line. Bob Wineburg, now 56, but who at the age of 14 won the city-wide junior high school foul shooting championship in Utica, New York, drilled a series of foul shots; it was the calmest any of us had seen Wineburg in years.

Game three turned out to be another story. We played a team from Charlotte ("Never too Late")—their pre-game rep was that one of their many good, big, players is the brother of Walter Davis,

The next year, we win bronze.

former UNC and NBA star (Walter, not the brother). They made our "big" men (57-year-old Rob Luisana, 6'1", our team captain, and 56-year-old Tally Mitchell, also 6'1"), look small. But, they had lost to the Pinehurst Hip and Knee Bobcats, the team we had beaten in our first game, so we assumed we could beat them. Maybe we could, but not that day. We stayed close for a while, trailing by four at the half. But they were big, they managed to get the ball inside to their big men, we kept fouling them, and they kept hitting their foul shots. (Unbecoming and whiny as it sounds, we were getting clobbered and fouls were not called. Unlike in the first two games, when our quickness got us to the foul line a lot, we barely got to the foul line in this game, though we should have). The bottom fell out midway through the second half when Never Too Late began to drain three-point shots—they must have hit six or seven in a five-minute span. We got clobbered. (We do not blame this loss on our coach, Frank Hatchett, a regular participant in the geezer game but who, at a mere 42 years of age, is much too young to play on Dead Men Dribbling. Coach Hatchett, who drove down that morning from Greensboro to coach us, last year coached the junior varsity at Greensboro Day to a 31-1 record. Therefore, our 2-1 record lowered his lifetime winning percentage. Neither John Wooden nor Dean Smith could have saved us in game three).

Three of the four teams in our bracket went 2-1 (the other was 0-3), but only two could move on to play in the next round the next morning. Because this was determined by point differential, and because we lost our third game 48-32, we were out. As it turned out, our bracket-mates did well: "Never Too Late" came in second in the tournament, and the "Pinehurst Hip and Knee Bobcats" came in third.

Tired and hungry, we ate dinner, during which we went over every play of each of the three games, and then drove back to Greensboro, talking about next year.

Appendix 2E. "Geezer game: Playing together for 31 years" by Robert Bell[5]

IT'S LUNCHTIME on a sunny December afternoon when the game begins at Guilford College's Ragan-Brown Field House. Outside, a warm spell has pushed the temperature close to 60, and lovers walk hand-in hand across the campus. Inside, there's a different romance going on: Ten guys going at it in a game of full-court basketball, which would be unremarkable except they're all old enough to be somebody's grandfather.

Some guys hit their 50s or 60s and take up golf. Others, the only exercise they manage is lifting themselves from the dinner table.

The guys at Ragan-Brown show up three times a week and run up and down the court for more than an hour, knowing it's a cheap, wonderful tonic for the ravages of old age.

"I always wondered what I'd be doing when I got, you know, closer to retirement," says Dan McCoy, 56 and a regular in the so-called "geezer game" each week. "This was not what I thought I'd be doing."

Yet here he is playing basketball with a dozen or so other middle-aged guys who love the game and can't give it up. The guys (and gals) include Richie Zweigenhaft, 62, who started these pickup games 31 years ago; Bob Wineburg, 57 and cancer-free for five years now; and Claire Morse, 62, who grew up playing the game way back when and has been unable to shake its pull since.

Watch them for a while and you see this is the basketball of pick-and-rolls, hook shots, two-handed set shots and running one-handers. This is basketball from another era, the game set in sepia. This is basketball before ESPN. Before the between-the-legs dribbling and the monster dunks of today's game—even before the jump shot, really.

5. Bell, Robert. 2007. "Geezer Game: Playing Together for 31 Years." *News & Record*, December 22. (https://www.greensboro.com/sports/geezer-game/article_5e1ff224-afa2-57c4-92f2-72ca69951b62.html)

"It's the game we grew up with," says 58-year-old Rob Luisana, another player. "It's the only one we know." Zweigenhaft says younger guys are allowed to play, provided they adhere to two rules: They must pass the ball, and they must be willing to play defense. "That usually eliminates a lot of guys," Zweigenhaft says. "But some catch on and enjoy it. It's like a whole new game has opened up to them."

Frank Hatchett, 46, took his game to Guilford College when his health club closed a few years back. He started for three years at Greensboro Day School, where he was an all-state player. He figured he could teach the old guys some new tricks. "I found out quickly they weren't pushovers," Hatchett says. "My first game with them I was thinking: Hey, these guys actually pass to each other. They cut through the lane. They're constantly looking for the open man."

Zweigenhaft says: "We play a different game than the one they play on the street nowadays."

And they play it well. Last month, five of the players finished third at the North Carolina Senior Games, playing three-on-three half-court basketball.

Zweigenhaft, a psychology professor at Guilford, organized the first pickup game in 1976 at Alumni Gym, affectionately known on campus as the "crackerbox" where Lloyd Free and M.L. Carr played for the Quakers.

The pickup players consisted of Guilford faculty and former YMCA members (the school once was affiliated with the Spears YMCA). Thirty-one years later, some guys have moved, some have retired and a few have died, but the geezer game is going strong every Monday, Wednesday and Friday—Sundays at Grimsley High School if the guys have any energy left.

Thirty-one years is a long time for anything. Even Zweigenhaft is surprised the games have endured. "There's been a whole new generation of players who have come in and stayed with it," he says. "I don't think it's the competition that keeps guys (coming back) as

Bob Wineburg (right) guards Richie Zweigenhaft (left) during a basketball game at Guilford College in Greensboro, NC, Friday, December 21, 2007.

much as it is the camaraderie." As the group's self-proclaimed commissioner, Zweigenhaft annually nominates someone for comeback player of the year. Four years ago, Wineburg seemed a lock for the award because he was recovering from prostate cancer. Instead, he lost out to 66-year-old Steve Schlehuser, who nearly died on the operating table that year. "We play through our injuries," Zweigenhaft jokes.

Many of the players say they feel the pain of their games when they get back to work. But none of them is about to trade in those aches for a rocking chair.

"My wife says she expects to get a call one day saying I've died on the basketball court," McCoy says. "If that happens, she'll know I died happy."

REFERENCES

Sources

Appenzeller, Herb. 1987. *Pride in the Past.* Greensboro, NC: Guilford College.

Bell, Robert. 2007. "Geezer Game: Playing Together for 31 Years." *News & Record*, December 22. (https://www.greensboro.com/sports/geezer-game/article_5e1ff224-afa2-57c4-92f2-72ca69951b62.html)

Bourdieu, Pierre. 1986. "The Forms of Capital." Pp. 241–58 in Handbook of theory and research for the sociology of education, edited by J. G. Richardson. New York, NY: Greenwood Press.

Chappelow, Craig. 2000. "Order on the Court: A Lesson in Leadership." *Leadership in Action* 20(5):14.

Luisana, Rob. 2006. "Men Score at Senior Games." *News & Record*, January 16, 10–12.

Morse, Claire. 1985. "The Committee Meeting: Guilford's Noontime Basketball." *Guilford Review* 22(Fall):19.

Springsteen, Bruce. 2016. *Born to Run.* New York, NY: Simon and Schuster.

Zweigenhaft, Richie. 2004. "Making Rags Out of Riches: Horatio Alger and the Tycoon's Obituary." *Extra! The Magazine of FAIR— the Media Watch Group*, 27–28.

Zweigenhaft, Richie. 2010. "Is This Curriculum for Sale?" *Academe*, 38–39.

Some Other Articles About Geezer Games

IT TURNS OUT that we are not the only long-running game, or game that includes mostly geezers. Every year or two friends send me articles they have seen about geezers playing ball for 25 years, for 30 years... None, so far, as long as our game has lasted. Here are references to a few of the articles I have received.

Breslow, Peter. 2016. "Friendships And Fractures: 30 Years of Pickup Basketball." *Weekend Edition*. (https://www.npr.org/2016/01/09/462246252/friendships-and-fractures-30-years-of-pickup-basketball)

Fried, Stephen. 2017. "Half-Court at Midlife: What I've Learned Playing Hoops with the Same Guys for 25 Years." *Philadelphia Magazine*, July 1. (https://www.phillymag.com/news/2017/07/01/half-court-basketball-league).

Jared, Scott. 2019. "Over Four Decades Woolen Knights Net Wins and Friends." *The Well*. (https://www.unc.edu/discover/over-four-decades-woollen-knights-net-wins-and-friends)

Kalish, Bob. 2013. "Geezer Basketball: At Age 72, a Parkinson's Patient Plays in a Pickup Game at the Y with Fellow 'Geezers' and Some Middleschoolers, Too." *Boston Globe*, August 18. (https://www.bostonglobe.com/magazine/2013/08/17/playing-basketball-with-parkinson/PxkpIaXNvPbkIpgpcgRQXO/story.html)

ACKNOWLEDGMENTS

A LOT OF PEOPLE helped me with this project, whether they knew it or not. Among those are (in reverse alphabetical order, by surname—as my students well know, alphabet liberation is one of my many causes):

Lisa Young, for her editorial suggestions on this manuscript, for her ongoing support in every way, and her general good advice, especially "friendship first!"

Dave Walters, Sports Information Director extraordinaire, for his help with sports data throughout the years, including some that landed in this book.

Rick Voigt, for listening to me talk about this project, but mainly I thank him so that he won't be too miffed about what I wrote in here about lawyers.

Jon Varnell, for the key role he played in getting my name on the court.

Deanna Thompson, for her valuable editorial guidance based on reading an earlier draft of this book.

Mark Stein, for his ongoing support and a lifetime of friendship, but also for coming up with the title of the book—the one I was using, much more academic and convoluted, was "From the Committee Meeting to the Geezer Game: How a Pickup Basketball Game Lasted for 44 Years (Sort of a Memoir)."

Andrew Saulters, for his invaluable savvy when it came to the formatting and design for this book.

Brian Lampkin, for what he has brought to the geezer game, for what he was brought to the broader Guilford community, and for his enthusiasm and support on this project.

Mike Gaspeny, for his steadfast friendship over the years, and for his thoughtful and incisive comments on an earlier draft of this book.

Gwen Erikson, for her help over the years on various of my writing projects, including some of the details about Guilford College included in the text of this book.

Liz Cook, for her helpful archival work on the dates of membership for two basketball-playing members of the Guilford Board of Trustees, Bruce Stewart and M. L. Carr.

Craig Chappelow, for his ongoing astute analyses of the geezer game, and also for the helpful ideas and editorial suggestions that he gave me, and for his enthusiasm, when I told him about this project.

Kent Chabotar, for that good Presidential decision in 2003.

Max Carter, for his love of basketball, his ongoing commitment to making the world a better place, and, more specifically, his helpful and encouraging thoughts about this project.

Kathy Adams, who, like Claire Morse (to whom this book is dedicated), was a valued colleague and is a treasured friend, for planting the suggestion, in just the right way and at just the right time, that I write something about the geezer game.

... and, last but not least (no longer reverse-alphabetically here), I want to thank the many geezers, past and current (long may you run).

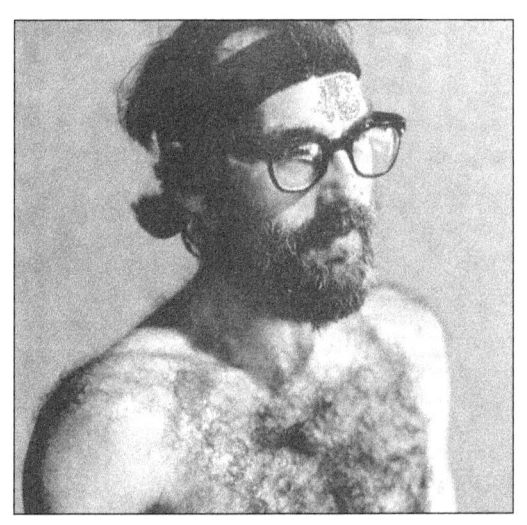

RICHIE ZWEIGENHAFT, Charles A. Dana Professor of Psychology at Guilford College, received his BA from Wesleyan University, his MA from Columbia University, and his Ph.D. from the University of California, Santa Cruz. He is the co-author (with G. William Domhoff) of a number of books on diversity in the American power structure and the co-editor (with Eugene Borgida) of a book on collaboration in psychological science. He is also the author or co-author of many academic articles and some articles that have appeared in more popular publications, including the *New York Times* and *Mother Jones*.

OPPOSITE, TOP. The Commish, 1988. From *The Quaker*.
OPPOSITE, BOTTOM. The Commish, 2015. Photo by Craig Chappelow.

www.ingramcontent.com/pod-product-compliance
Lightning Source LLC
Chambersburg PA
CBHW071409080526
44587CB00017B/3229